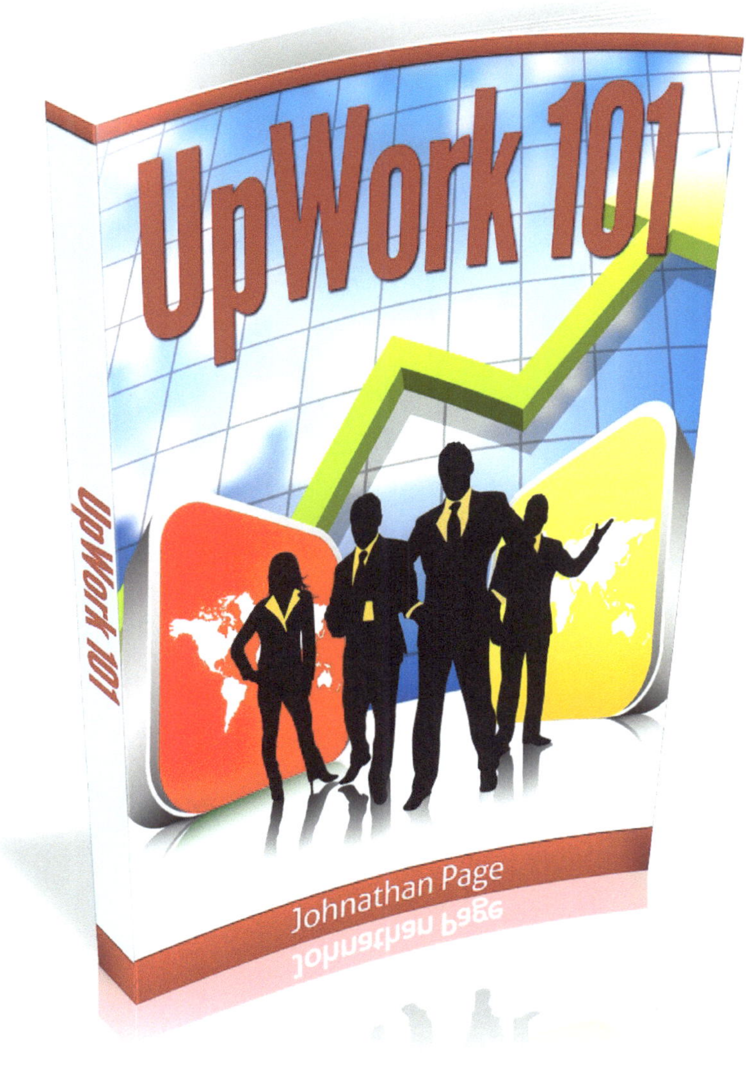
UpWork 101
UpWork 101
Johnathan Page

Contents

Chapter1 Introduction

What is Upwork?   4

Who can Join Upwork?   5

Who is a freelancer? And what is freelancing?   5

How Upwork makes money? 6

What Membership plan Upwork offers? 6

Chapter 2 Let's Get Started

How to join upwork?   9

How to make Account?   9

Chapter 3 Building profile and Finding work

    How to build your profile?   12

    What is Bidding and When to start Bidding?   17

    How to find work on upwork?   18

    Types of Projects on Upwork. 20

    Why is Upwork secure?   23

Chapter4 Submitting Proposals and Appearing in Interviews

    How to write a Job proposal. 24

    How to give an effective interview? 27

Chapter 5 Start Working and get Paid

    working on the assigned work   29

    Submit task   29

    Get Paid   29

    Repeating the cycle   30

Chapter6 How to be a successful Freelancer?

   Why freelancers face failures? 31

    How to be a successful freelancer? 33

Summary

Introduction

What Is Upwork ?

Odesk, or Elance, now called Upwork is a platform of online working. The C.E.O of it is Stephane Kasriel. It was introduced by him in the year 2003. It's a platform where people can work online even by staying at their home. The agencies, companies, businessman, experienced workers and skilled people from all over the world can communicate with each other on this platform and can work together in a better way.

Upwork makes it easy to find the right person, for the task on the right time accurately and more quickly. Both the client and the services provider deal with each other to achieve their purposes. It is easy to get send and receive payments quickly right after the completion of the contract. The freelancers don`t have to wait long for getting the payment of his or her services.

Who is a freelancer? And What is freelancing ?

A freelancer is a person who is self-employed. He or she doesn't work permanently for an organization or company for a long term. A freelancer may be an individual, or a number of persons forming an agency and working together on different projects according to their skills.

Freelancing is one of the easiest, fastest, and lowest cost ways to start working for you on different freelancing websites.

Who Can Join Upwork ?

Upwork is open to for all the firms, agencies, professionals and individual freelancers. A person in Australia providing the services of graphic designing, a freelancer from India providing the services of web development or an agency in England providing the services of writing, they all can join Upwork for their purposes. It's a global platform and has no boundaries.
Upwork is from one of the most top ranked platforms used for online working and liked by both the freelancers, clients and agencies.

Upwork Charges:-

Upwork makes money by charging a 10% Fee from the payment made on a single project. These charges are applied on both fixed and hourly rates. These service charges are taken from the freelancer.

For example: - If a freelancer takes a project of $100 then he will receive a total of $90 and the Upwork will get $10.

Upwork Membership Plans: -

Upwork is presently offering two membership plans. One is Basic and the other is Paid freelancer Plus Membership plan. These plans are offered to both the individual freelancers and agencies.

Freelancers Membership Plans :-

The Paid membership plan includes more benefits than the Basic one. The basic plan doesn't include any kind of charges and is free to use. It provides the freelancer and agency with all the necessary elements and functions which are needed to run the business. Those who want extra premium benefits they chose paid freelancer plus membership plan .This plain charges are $10 per month. All the users of Upwork either individual freelancers or agencies have to choose any of the membership plans before proceeding to the next steps of profile building.

In freelancer Basic plan 60 connects, hourly and fixed price protection is provided.

While in freelancer plus along with hourly and fixed price protection, 70 connects are provided. (Connects are usually the tokens which the freelancer uses while applying for a job post. A client also use connects in order to invite a freelancer to apply or if he/she wanted to re-hire the same freelancer which they have hired before). Not only this freelancer can also buy more connects. The cost for buying a single connect is $1. If they have some unused connects these connects will also be added into connects of the coming month. Using this membership plan also enables the freelancer to check the maximum, minimum and average bid of any job.

Agency Membership Plans:-

This again includes Basic and Plus membership plans.

The basic is free and the agency don't have to pay any charges for this plan. This plan is for one-person agency. The agency is free to show its logo and name in the profile. Just like freelancer basic plan it also included 60 connects per billing cycle.

AGENCY BASIC	AGENCY PLUS
Owner Only The agency owner applies for jobs and works as a one-person business, with no team members	**Multi-Person Teams** Add and support unlimited teams and team members
60 Connects per Month*	**80 Connects per Month*** Shared across the agency
Hourly Protection For eligible hourly jobs, you're ensured payment for every hour worked	**Rollover Connects** Unused Connects automatically carry over to the following month (up to 80)
Fixed Price Protection For fixed-price jobs, payments are secured through pre-funded milestones	**Buy Additional Connects** If you run out of Connects, you can buy more at any time ($1 per Connect)
	View Competitor Bids See the minimum, maximum, and average bid for any job
	Hourly Protection For eligible hourly jobs, you're ensured payment for every hour worked
***NOTE** Connects are used to apply for jobs, with each application requiring 1 to 5 Connects (0 if you're invited or rehired)	**Fixed-Price Protection** For fixed-price jobs, payments are secured through pre-funded milestones

While for plus membership plans the agency have to pay the charges of about $20 per month. This plan is used by multi-person agency and includes 80 connects per month. Not only this agency is also given the benefits of unlimited invitation to job, payment protection and the unused connects can be roll over up in the coming month.

Both the freelancers and agencies can change their membership plans in the future.

Chapter 2
Let`s Get Started

To start working on Upwork is very simple. We will guide you step by steps.

How to Join Upwork ?

To join Upwork is very easy and can be achieved in three simple steps: -

1. First Step is to sign up .If you haven`t signed, up then it's the right time to do this and choose a membership plan according to your needs and purposes.

2. Build your profile. Fill in all the options correctly.

3. Set a payment method for your account. By which way you want to send or receive payments in your account.

How to make Account ?

It is very easy to make account on Upwork. You must have a reliable and permanent internet connection.

In order to make account on Upwork one has to follow the following simple steps:

1. Visit www.upwork.com

2. Choose your category, either you want to use Upwork and start working as an individual freelancer or want to hire freelancers.

3. Third step is to fill the form and provide all the necessary information which is asked.

4. Choose the membership plan (the memberships plans are available for both the individual freelancers and agencies) either you want basic or Paid Freelancer Plus Membership plan.

5. After filling the form click on "get started".

6. You will receive a confirmation email from Upwork on your email address (the one you mentioned in the form) .Open your email, Click on the link provided by the Upwork Community.

Please verify your email address

Hi Elex,

Thanks for creating an account with Upwork. Click below to confirm your email address: https://www.upwork.com/signup/verify-email/token/~~452b65f7ac7456f3

If you have problems, please paste the above URL into your web browser.

Thanks,
Upwork Support

7. After the link is opened your account is confirmed.

8. Click on Create Profile and choose the category in which your skills best fit.

9. After choosing the main category select any 4 categories keeping in view your skills and the services you are going to provide.

10. The next step is to build your profile.

Chapter 3
Building Profile and Finding Work

After making an account, the next step is to build profile in such a way that it clearly shows each and everything about the freelancer. Freelancer's professional career, work history, professional title, skills, languages he speaks, and education history. After completing the profile you can star finding the job in your field.

How to Build your profile:-

Profile is very important. The profile needs to be complete 100%. You have to build the profile in such a way that it should stand out of others. It must be an impressive one and must give a professional look.

It will help you to get orders from the clients. So fill all the details accurately.

Overview :-

Overview is very important element in profile. The overview of a freelancer must be related to the services which he/she is offering. You don`t have to beat around the bushes. Just explain about your skills and services and highlight them as much as clear. While writing the overview don`t use short hand writing. Make complete sentences.

Everything should be crystal clear so and must be easy to understand. Don`t flower up the language too much make the things understandable.

Your profile must give the impression and reflection of the services you are going to provide.

So give your best while writing an overview. Freelancers also pay other freelance writers for writing an awesome overview for them.

Profile Picture :-

Profile picture should not be fake otherwise the Upwork team will not make your profile public. In case of any blunder in the profile picture the Upwork team will send you emails and will guide you about the area in which you did mistakes.

The profile picture must be a professional one and the face must be clear. Pictures with plain background gives a better view of the whole profile.

The agencies are free to use their logos on profile pictures.

Upwork Help Center: Action Required. Account flagged for policy violation   [People]

Cez Pangaibat (Upwork Help Center)
Jun 22, 5:45 AM

Dear Elex,

During our regular reviews of the Freelancer community I noticed that your profile image does not comply with the Upwork image policy as it needs to be a true likeness of you.

In addition, please revise your overview. In general, your overview should use complete sentences and clearly describe your skills and/or expertise. The skills noted should be related to your title.

Choosing the relevant Skills and Professional Title :-

While completing your profile you have to fill all the details, one of those is choosing the relevant skills and a professional title.

It is very important for a freelancer to be very careful and attentive while choosing the top three skills. They must be related to your services. Mentioning irrelevant skills will throw a bad impression on the mind of the viewer.

If your job title is about Visual Designer so the most appropriate skills to be mentioned are web design, brand consulting and graphic design. If a freelancer mentions here content writing below the title of Visual Designer, it doesn't make any sense, and gives a poor impression.

Take Skills Tests and Introductional Video :-

Upwork is providing a number of test for its users. These are available in the section of "Test".

Every freelancer must have to take the Upwork guideline test .To make sure that you have read our upwork manual. After this the freelancer may search for the test about the field which they have chosen.

Skill Tests

Demonstrate your abilities to prospective clients by completing skills tests in your areas of expertise

Tests for you
- U.S. Academic Writing Test
  Duration: 40 minutes
- Online Article Writing and Blogging Test (UK Version)
  Duration: 40 minutes
- Online Article Writing and Blogging Test (U.S. Version)
  Duration: 40 minutes
- Creative Writing Test - Non-fiction (UK Version)
  Duration: 40 minutes

Take 3 or 4 tests related to your skills so that when the client visits your profile he may know about your knowledge.

Taking tests also help the freelancer to know what kind of information is necessary for the title which you used and are you compatible with this or not.

You can also make a video and let the client know about yourself, skills and services you are going to provide. But again you have to be very relevant when talking about all this. Don`t explain in deep details about yourself, in fact your main focus will be about your profession and services. The client has no interest in your personal life so do not elaborate it.

Work Employment History:-

If the freelancer has worked before on some other platform (either online or at some company offline) he may mention it in this category. This also gives a very good impression. Start adding the past work experiences from the most recent to the older ones. For fresh users who haven't done any job or task before they may leave this category, this also gives a very good impression.

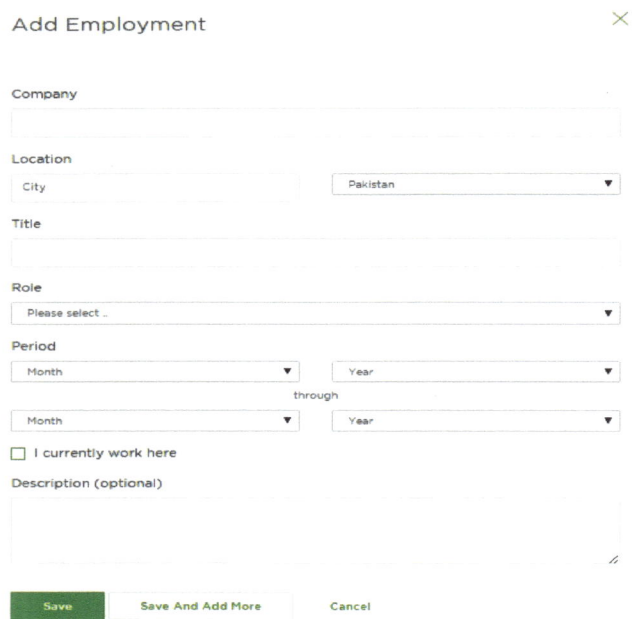

Education, Achievements and Certificates:-

Add your most recent education and show about your accomplishments. This helps the freelancer to make others know how much hard working he/she is .He/she may also attach any of their professional certificates related to the job title.

If the Professional title is about Graphic designing and the freelancer has attach a certificate about the game "chess" then it's wrong. These both things have nothing to do with each other.

What is Bidding and When to start Bidding?

Applying for the job is called as bidding on Upwork. The right time to start bidding is right after the completion of your profile.

One you have completed the profile and sent for review. Upwork team will review it and then tell you whether you can start bidding or not.

If the profile is approved by Upwork the freelancer can start bidding on various jobs. For bidding you need connects which will be provided on the basis of which membership plan you have chosen.

Promote your Account:-

One of the ways to find the work is to promote your account in your social circle and on social media websites.

There is a chance that your profile may reach to the professionals and agency and they may hire you .You can also link your account to other sites like google+ , Facebook, LinkedIn, twitter and many others .

How to find work on upwork?

Once your profile is complete, and approved by Upwork team you can start searching for job in "job feed". Job feed will show a number of job offers which are given by the clients and agencies. You don't necessary have to bid on all the jobs but have to find those jobs in which you think you can work best and provide the client with quality work. For finding the right job you have to set your search preferences.

You have to choose the right category in job feed which you have mentioned in your professional title, then you have to choose the work categories according to you core skills which you mentioned in your profile. By doing this the Upwork job feed will show you all the jobs related to your chosen preferences.

While applying for the job you must have to check that either the client's or agency payment method is verified or not .If it is verified then you may apply for this job. If they payment method is not verified then don't go for this job because it's a bluff.

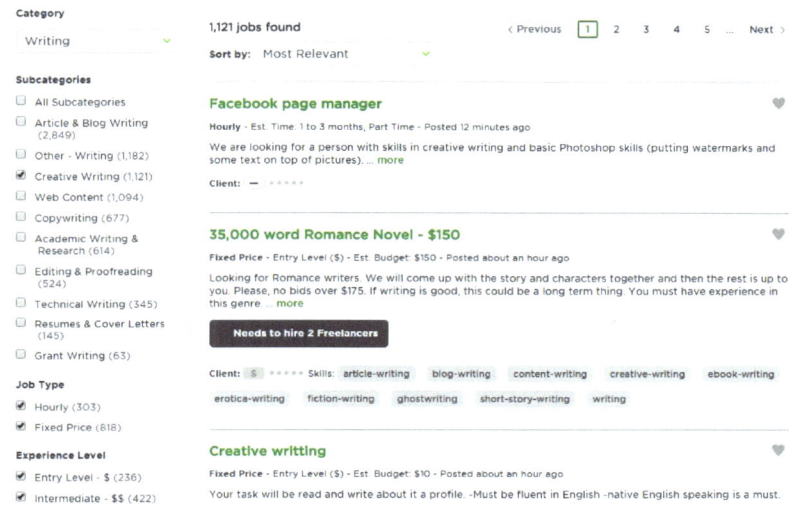

Therefore, these details are shown to all the freelancers in order to make them secure about what they are going to do.

As shown in the above picture you can search for both job types.

A freelancer can chose more than one category while searching for the job. If you have marked only for "Creative Writing" then Upwork will show job posts only related to creative writing. If you have marked both "Creative writing" and "Academic Writing" then Upwork will show job posts related to the categories respectively.

Types of Projects on upwork: -

The projects on Upwork are of mainly of two types. These are:-

1. Fixed Price Contracts

2. Hourly Price Contracts

Hourly Price Contracts:-

In these contracts the freelancer is paid on the basis of hours. These contracts are preferred for those services which can easily be completed within the defined hours.

Before starting to work on hourly based contracts the freelancer and client must agree and decide about the authorized hours on the offers detail page.

If the freelancer agrees to work on a hourly basis and the client agrees to pay for the hourly work of the freelancer then it is very necessary for the freelancer to install the Upwork team app. The app helps to track your project hours while you are working. It will take snap shots of the freelancer's screen after every 10 minute intervals when he is working on the project assign to him. Those screen shots will be as a proof with the freelancer that he has done the work in the hour which was decided by both the parties (freelancer and client or agency) before.

Incase when the task is not completed within the decided time then the freelancer can show those screen shots to client. These screen shots will help the freelancer in order to tackle any kind of dispute if arises by the client. As a result the freelancer will be paid for his services. So the Team app is very important for those working on hourly based contracts.

Before processing the payment the client will review the freelancers' timelogs. The billing cycle ends every Sunday and the payments become available after 10 Days of time.

Fixed Price Contracts: -

In fixed price contracts the amount to be paid for a single project is fixed. The client and freelancer make the deal on a fixed amount .The freelancer has to clear about when to submit the project, what to submit and how much he will charge for his services. The client has to make the freelancer aware about the deadlines and about the work which he wants from the freelancer.

The projects well suited for fixed price contracts are of graphic designing, web development and mobile app development.

The work must be submitted to the client using the Upwork platform.

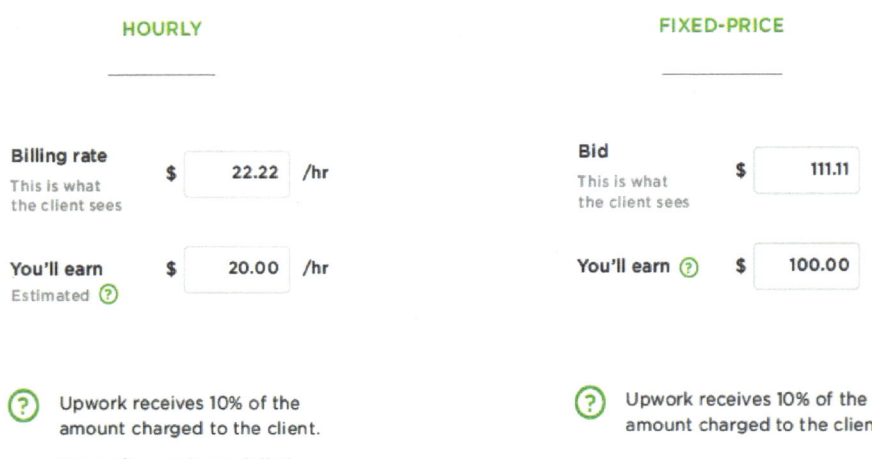

Escrow and milestone based payments :-

In fixed price contracts both freelancer and the client will make a list of milestones. In this the client will prefund each milestone and the money will be visibly held on the Upwork platform. When the freelancer is done with the work, he will let the client know about the work using the Upwork platform. If the client is satisfied with the work they will send you the payments which was fixed before, but if they are not satisfied with the work of the freelancer then both the client and freelancer will discuss with each other about the work. If the issue still not solved then they may ask the Upwork team for free dispute assistance. And Upwork will schedule a moderate discussion and come to a mutually agreeable decision and come to a conclusion about releasing the funds from Escrow.

Why is Upwork Secure?

Upwork has various payment protection programs which provide security to both the clients, agencies and individual freelancers about their payments. It builds the trust of the agencies and freelancers to use this platform. That is why Upwork is getting popularity after each passing day. The number of users is increasing day by day.

The fixed price protection is protected by the fixed contract managed by the escrow and milestones. The user just has to set the terms, send the work using the Upwork platform and he/she can have the confidence that you will get paid.

In addition in hourly based work Upwork also takes action if either a freelancer cheats the agency or if the client tricks or don`t give the freelancer his right payment. In this case the victim send complain to Upwork against the bluff creator and Upwork after noticing the minute details of the event gives the solution. In some cases we also suspend the account cheater.

Upwork is considered as a secure medium because it enables the user to set various security questions for his account. Thus, increasing the protection level of user`s account.

Chapter4

Submitting Proposals and Appearing in Interviews

The competition in each field is increasing day by day. Similarly the number of users on Upwork is increasing .So in order to get job on Upwork you have to write the best covering letter.

Writing a Job Proposal:-

While applying for a job the thing which matters the most after profile is the covering letter.

Most of the clients have asked about the cover letters. Through this they came to know about the freelancer's skills, services and his working experience.

Cover letter is your marketing area .How much and how better you advertise about yourself. The best you write the cover letter the more your chances will increase to be selected by the client. You have to mention your skills according to the job description which the client has mentioned. Any irrelevant skills or job experienced if mentioned will make a poor impression and the client will not consider you to be hired.

Different clients ask different questions when you apply for a job, so try to answer all the questions in a better way. Let the client know why they should hire you through your cover letter.

Following are some of tips about how to write a cover letter that will make it easy for your to get selected for the interview and then to be hired.

1. Be very precise and to the point about mentioning your skills, and past experiences. Don't elaborate too much, be specific, because your clients don't have enough time to read long stories. They just want to know about your eligibility to be hired or not by looking at your experience and skills.

2. The client likes it when freelancer shows interest in the job. Ask questions from your client if anything is unclear to you. Tell your client about how can you bring quality in the client's project.

3. Most of the freelancers copy and paste the same cover letter and apply for different jobs. Clients in order to check whether the freelancer has read the job post completely or not mentions some key words or ask questions which the freelancer has to mention too and answer while writing a covering letter. So, make sure that your cover letter is not a copy and paste one, and follow the instructions attentively.

4. Tell the client why specifically you are interested in the task.

5. Outline what you can walk through the door and deliver.

6. Don't think about what the client is going offer you for the task, but think what value you can bring into the task and show you this thinking in your cover letter.

7. Showcase your skills more than your education.

8. Be real and normal don't exaggerate too much.

9. The last step while apply for the job is to check whether you have set the right rate (both hourly and fixed), are there any grammatical mistakes? (If yes then correct), proof read the covering letter and answers of the questions once again. Have you attached the samples of your work (if requested)? After checking all these details then hit on "send".

Got an interview Call?

After applying for the job, you may get a call for the interview by the client. This is not the case all the time. May be the client directly hires someone else. If he/she hires someone else then you will get the notification that "Your job for---- is declined". The client is not responsible to respond each and every freelancer individually.

How to give your best in Interview:-

After founding your covering letter and skills interesting the client invites you for an interview. Try to give him/her response immediately and set a time which suits both the parties. Make sure that your system is working well and the place where you are sitting is peaceful, because any type of noises if going by your side will disappoint the client .Now, it's the time to take the project from him/her. There are few tips which help you to give the best interview: -

1. Let the client decide about the interview timing and platform, whether it is on Skype or on a cell phone or any other medium. You must open heartedly have to accept his decisions about this.

2. In interview he/she may ask you few questions related to your skills and the project. So, make sure before going for interview you have searched on the topic and have noted few answers about the technical parts of the project so that you both have a meaning full conversation.

3. If you find some difficulties in the project after it is being fully told by the clients then do tell him but don`t miss guide the client otherwise it leads to a bad experience for both the client and freelancer. Be honest, while answering, if you don`t know the answer of anything then say it openly.

4. Behave like a professional freelancer, tell the client about your skills,

achievements and work experience.

5. Your reason for wanting the project must be clear. Ask yourself before the final interview why you applied for the particular job? Only you better know the answer of this. Just because you applied for the job because its rate is high or you are looking for some work is not the reason that the client will hire you. But tell the clients what value you can bring in the project and how much you know about the task.

6. Time is critical and matters a lot. You must be be online 10 minutes before the interview.

7. In the end of the interview don`t forget to thank him for considering your application for the job.

8. If he has asked for certain details during the interview don`t forget to send.

Chapter5
Start Working and Get Paid

Work sincerely for the person or company. The more you work sincerely the more you get success.

Working on the assigned work:-

Once you are successful in the interview and the client has assigned you the task .The next step is to start working on it. You have to keep in mind all the term and the instructions the client has provided you for the project. If you will not follow any of the instructions then your project will not be rated as good by the client. So try to be a responsible freelancer and provided accuracy in your work and it must be error free.

Submitting the task:-

If you fail to submit the task on time then the client may cancel the deal even if u have completed it later or sometimes he/she may accepts it (depending on the client) .But as far as the freelancer is concerned so he/she must submit the task on time.

Get Paid: -

The final and the last step is that the freelancer is paid after completing the project assigned to him/her. The payments may be hourly based or fixed, depends on the type the freelancer has chosen for the project.

Repeating the cycle: -

You are done with the task assigned to you and had got the payment. Login in to your account again. The next step is to start bidding again, write covering letter according to the job description and keeping in mind the client's instructions .hope for getting the interview call and get selected.

Log in and get to work

Username or Email

Password

Log in   ☐ Remember me next time

i) Apply for a job   ii) Appear in interview (optional depends on client)
iii) Take the task   iv) Understand it well
v) Submit the task   vi) Get paid again & SO On....

Chapter6

How to be a successful Freelancer

Now, trends are changing. Now a day's people are more interested in working as a freelancer. Freelancing is a freedom of working. You work on your own choice. There is no boss to keep an evil eye on you. You work according to your mood and choices. You are your own boss.

All the freelancers don't succeed some face failures and some enjoy success. But both failure and success is not a permanent thing. You find to first find the problem and then the solution of your troubles. So, let us discuss about few major points related to why a freelancer fails or succeeds.

Why Freelancer Face failures:-

No one gets success very rapidly and early in any field .You have to go through up and downs, hardships and face different barriers which come between you and your success. Freelancers face failures most of the time due to following reasons: -

1. Beginners always get disappointed when they don`t get any task. Even after six or seven months they don`t came across any good news. The problem is the

proposal letter which they write is not of a standard to get the clients attention.

2. Most of the time, they are copy pasting the same covering letter for all the jobs and not following the instruction of the client which he mentions in the job description. By this the client came to know that you haven't read about the job completely and he/she rejects you.

3. The freelancer fails to give his best in the interview due to lack of knowledge about the related job for which he applied.

4. Freelancers don't know how to sell their selves. Those who fail to do self branding can do nothing. You have to do the marketing of your own self in order to catch the attention of the clients.

5. When you fail for the first time, you are de-motivated, but that's not the end, one has to learn from the mistakes. Allowing fear to control your feelings is the beginning of failure. Once you are de-motivated, you will definitely not be able to complete your work.

6. Poor communication skills also make your chances less to grab the project from the client. So work on making your communication skills good and understandable.

7. Freelancers face failure because they fail to set the rate according to the client's budget. Due to which the client keeping his budget in his mind, rejects to give the project to the freelancer.

8. You don't work on the task when the clients wants you to revise it again.

9. Your skills are not developed fully and you started working. The freelancer before getting full command over his/her skills stars working, and when he fails to provide the client the quality work he fails.

10. Your heart is not in the task assigned to you. You don't know about your actually skills and start working on the task which you saw others doing.

How to be a successful freelancer?

Different rules work for different kind of people. All the people are not the same and so does their skills and personalities. Changing the face cannot change anything but facing the change can change everything.

In order to be a successful freelancer you have to simply follow the following strategies.

1. The first step should be you must have a complete, approved profile. The things should be clear (Professionals title, skills, samples, experience history etc).Freelancers having 100% complete account details are having more chances of getting task then from those who have incomplete profiles.

2. Start working from low rates. In the start as you are new on upwork so the client don't know about you. Because there will be no ratings on your profile by which the client assume that you are worth to be worked with. First try to work on lower rates and grab as many projects as you can. Give the best work to clients so that

they give you positive ratings and your profile will start upgrading. After this you can raise you rate according to the work.

3. Don`t show any kind of attitude or rude behavior to the clients. Be polite with your clients so that they give you the task the next time as well.

4. Talk to as many people in your daily life as you can. By this you will know about different people .This will build confidence in you and you will learn how to deal with different clients.

5. Work when you are at work. Be sincere with the task given to you. Don't do other activities while doing the task. Your full attention will be towards the project.

6. Try to meet with the deadlines. You have to be very much punctual and responsible. Time is money and you will see you a single second matters a lot when you show delay in submitting a project.

7. As the number of freelancers is increasing day by day. So, I order to compete in this you have to attract your client by giving him certain advantages in the form of discounts.

8. Whenever you start providing a new services, send a message to your previous clients and let them know about this. May be they are looking for the same services somewhere else.

9. Try to manage time, for each project, make a schedule and divide the work on time and then work accordingly.

10. Learn to say NO, for the work about which you don't knows but don't do unfair with the client. A single negative feedback from a client will put a bad image on your career.

11. Set a different rate when you are working for an individual client and an organization. Set lower rates when working for an individual client as you have to keep in mind the clients budget as well. When working for an organization you may increase your rate.

12. When your clients ask for revision instead of saying "No" or placing lame excuse you should work on his/her request. The clients greatly appreciate it and it is also a form of showing respect for the client.

13. You must be hardworking and striving. To get good is not as easy as it seems to be. Sometimes you have to burn the night oil as well to get success.

14. Communicate with people of same profession as yours and build a network with them. Two heads are always better than one.

15. Learn to work in a competitive environment.

16. Try to be transparent with the person you are working with. Either it's an organization, company or individual client. Show your interest in them and there business. A client always wanted to know if he is hiring someone and giving his/her money so who is that person? So be sure to inject who you are into your brand.

17. Whatever you are getting for providing your services. Save a little of the entire income.

18. Try to be creative and show uniqueness in your work

19. Practice, practice and practice matters a lot. You cannot design or give the best at your first time. You have to do lot of work and practice to achieve success in something. Practice makes a man perfect.

20. When you are done with the task assigned to you, ask for feedback. You don`t realize about your weak points and errors in your work as quickly as others .Other perform this job of finding mistake better. This will give you a best chance to improve yourself. Not only this, but the client also felt important. Getting someone else's opinion is always good and this will help you to become even more successful.

Summary

This book is a complete guide about Upwork and how to get success on Upwork. Upwork is a platform where everyone can showcase their selves. Advertise about their skills and services and can find job. Freelancers earn money by doing work. Companies and clients get their task done by giving money to freelancers. The Upwork earns money by charging on each project that freelancer gets. The objectives of all the users are achieved in a better way. The user don`t have to pay any kind of charges while making the account. It's totally free. But when the freelancer or agency wants to get premium benefits then they have to buy them and chose the premium memberships plan.

Upwork provides security to both the freelancer and clients by providing different payments protection methods. Work on the tips and get success. Try to overcome your week points. Grow your business more and more. Make milestones for yourself and break those milestones.

Best of luck!

www.ingramcontent.com/pod-product-compliance
Lightning Source LLC
Chambersburg PA
CBHW041151180526
45159CB00002BB/777